D1416965

Desert Animals

Lizards

by Emily Rose Townsend

banded gecko

Consulting Editor: Gail Saunders-Smith, Ph.D.

Consultant: Michael A. Mares, Ph.D.
Director, Sam Noble Oklahoma Museum
of Natural History, University of Oklahoma
Norman, Oklahoma

Pebble Books

an imprint of Capstone Press
Mankato, Minnesota

Pebble Books are published by Capstone Press
151 Good Counsel Drive, P.O. Box 669, Mankato, Minnesota 56002
http://www.capstone-press.com

1 2 3 4 5 6 08 07 06 05 04 03

Library of Congress Cataloging-in-Publication Data
Townsend, Emily Rose.
    Lizards / by Emily Rose Townsend.
    p. cm.—(Desert animals)
    Includes bibliographical references (p. 23) and index.
    Contents: Lizards—Body—Deserts—What lizards do.
    ISBN 0-7368-2077-9 (hardcover)
    1. Lizards—Juvenile literature. [1. Lizards.] I. Title.
QL666.L2 T68 2004
597.95—dc21   2002154584

Summary: Simple text and photographs describe lizards that live in deserts.

Note to Parents and Teachers

The Desert Animals series supports national science standards
related to life science. This book describes and illustrates lizards
that live in desert regions. The photographs support early readers in
understanding the text. The repetition of words and phrases helps
early readers learn new words. This book also introduces early
readers to subject-specific vocabulary words, which are defined in
the Glossary section. Early readers may need assistance to read
some words and to use the Table of Contents, Glossary, Read More,
Internet Sites, and Index/Word List sections of the book.

Table of Contents

4

Lizards

Lizards are reptiles.
Most lizards have
short legs and long tails.

Clark's spiny lizard

Body

Lizards are cold-blooded.
Their body temperature
changes with the
air temperature.

short-horned lizard

8

Lizards can be many
sizes and colors.
They have scaly skin.

collared lizard

Deserts

Many lizards live in deserts. Lizards rest in the sun until the sun warms their bodies.

white-throated savanna monitor

deserts where lizards live

Lizards live in every desert in the world. Many lizards live in deserts in the United States and South America.

What Lizards Do

Some lizards eat
other animals. Some
lizards eat plants.

Gila monster

Some lizards eat insects. They catch insects with their long, sticky tongues.

shovel-nosed lizard

18

Many lizards change colors to hide from predators.

Texas horned lizard

Most lizards can run fast to escape predators.

collared lizard

Glossary

desert—an area that is very dry; deserts do not get much rainfall.

escape—to avoid or get away from

predator—an animal that hunts other animals for food; predators of lizards include hawks, roadrunners, foxes, coyotes, and snakes.

reptile—a cold-blooded animal that crawls or creeps on the ground; some reptiles also live in trees or in the water.

scaly—having scales; scales are small pieces of hard skin that cover a lizard's body.

temperature—the measure of how hot or cold something is

Read More

Murray, Julie. *Lizards.* Animal Kingdom. Edina, Minn.: Abdo Publishing, 2003.

Robinson, Fay. *Amazing Lizards!* Hello Science Reader! New York: Scholastic, 1999.

Schaefer, Lola M. *What Is a Reptile?* Animal Kingdom. Mankato, Minn.: Pebble Books, 2001.

Internet Sites

Do you want to find out more about lizards? Let FactHound, our fact-finding hound dog, do the research for you.

Here's how:

1) Visit *http://www.facthound.com*

2) Type in the **Book ID** number: **0736820779**

3) Click on **FETCH IT**.

FactHound will fetch Internet sites picked by our editors just for you!

Index/Word List

Word Count: 106
Early-Intervention Level: 13

Editorial Credits
Mari C. Schuh, editor; Patrick D. Dentinger, designer; Kelly Garvin, photo researcher;
Karen Risch, product planning editor

Photo Credits
A. Blank/Bruce Coleman Inc., 18
Bob & Clara Calhoun/Bruce Coleman Inc., 6
Comstock Klips, 12
Dwight R. Kuhn, 1
Joe McDonald/Tom Stack & Associates, 4
Joe McDonald, 8, 20
Robin Brandt, 10
Visuals Unlimited/Joe McDonald, cover, 16; Jim Merli, 14